Rest & Receive
The Cover and Comfort of a God Who Never Leaves Us

A devotional by
Justine Froelker

Cover illustration: Emily Baker
Cover design: Elizabeth Ferris and Justine Froelker
All rights reserved.
ISBN: 978-0-9989875-2-1

DEDICATION

To my community who took up the sword for me, who bombarded Heaven with me, who added commas, who said 'me too' and 'I'm here', and most of all, who helped me see, feel, and know God was in this battle by loving me like Jesus.

To those who have forgotten, never known, or want more of the endless, reckless, ever wooing, all encompassing, never changing, never ever leaving love and comfort of Father, Son, and Spirit.

TABLE OF CONTENTS

ACKNOWLEDGMENTS

To say that my book projects are a community effort is always an understatement. I am so thankful to my friends, team, and community for their support in comma addition, prayers, cover ideas, encouragement, and general love. This miracle of a book would not have been possible without my fellow warriors who love faithfully, believe fiercely, and live courageously.

Most of all, this wild, crazy, scary, and nearly impossible book would not be here without a God who made sure I felt Him in the darkest of dark, who opened my eyes to see, and who loves with grace-filled abandon.

May you meet, see, and feel Him in these words too.

Welcome

Introduction

For several years now I have prayed, breathed, and asked for a word or verse at the end of the year to guide my way in the coming year.

A word of intention.
A verse to light the way forward.

This year you could say I was a little confused about what God showed me as He gave me a phrase instead.

The threshing floor.

Um, what?

With a little research I soon discovered the threshing floor is a place where the harvest is worked. It is the place where Ruth was loved again. Some say it is the place where good and evil will be separated, such as in the wheat being separated from the chaff so the wind can carry it away. It is the place of the overflow of God's goodness.

It wouldn't take long for God to meet me on the threshing floor in what would be the toughest year of my life, like for so many others, the year 2020. And toughest not only for the very obvious reasons of the brutal uncertainty and plain hard of the year.

For me it began with a severe allergic reaction to medications where I truly felt like I was going to die.

I had to fight for my life.

Much of the fight was on my knees in prayer.
Begging.
And yes praising.

And God met me.

He met me with His cover and comfort.
He met me with His provision, protection, promises, and presence.

And as crazy as it sounds, He met me on the threshing floor in some of the most vivid visions of my life.

And they kept coming, most often in a health battle that was unexpected and difficult, which without a doubt has also been a mighty spiritual battle with very earthly pain.

The common thread in all the visions was a phrase He kept searing into my knowing, often upon the threshing floor,
Show Me to Them.

So, my brave friends, that is what you are holding in your hands now.

This is a collection of visions from God to help you feel, find, and receive the cover and comfort of our loving Father.

It sounds crazy.
And it isn't.

Will you join me even if it is?

An Invitation

Throughout 2020, especially during active health struggles where my pain felt unbearable, I started taking rests in the afternoons. I've never been much of a napper, or rester for that matter. Recovering striver and hustler over here, as I raise my hand, anyone else? It took a brutal season to get me to stop and rest in His presence. Many days this is simply 20 to 40 minutes where I lay on the couch flanked by my three little dogs taking deep breaths and inviting God in. Some days it is in the ten minutes waiting to be seen by a doctor or receiving treatments.

Soon my days didn't feel complete without this time, as my soul slowly and surely became not so weary.

And quickly, God started showing me the visions you will read in this book.

My hope and prayer is that God will meet you in these vision devotionals.

Most of all, my prayer is that you create and receive a bit of time to pause and meet Him.

To rest in the presence of our Father, Son, and Spirit.

A few notes first:

Whenever I am referring to anything God, Jesus, or Holy Spirit I write with uppercase letters.

When I am writing about the enemy, satan, or anything darkness, I use lowercase letters. Frankly, he doesn't deserve any honor, even that of a capital letter for his name.

Finally, to me, Holy Spirit is a person and not a thing, and therefore I do not write the Holy Spirit, but rather Holy Spirit.

Here we go...
Come on in child and rest.

Maybe you can only make ten minutes a day, will you still join me?

I'll even take five.

Not even sure how to start?

Here are a few things that have helped me to pause, invite God in, and simply rest and be. More often than not, the following breath prayers are how I begin my afternoon rests, also called my Jesus vision naps.

First, grab a pen and paper and pause to think about how God, Jesus, and Holy Spirit show up for you. They are three in one and one in three, I know, still pretty mind-blowing. Still, knowing who they each are to you can help guide your quiet time. For example, for me:

- God feels like the all-powerful, creative genius, and loving Father.
- Jesus is my empathic friend who knows suffering and struggle and also is the miraculous Healer.
- Holy Spirit is the creative, joy-filled, fun, breath, that leads and feels, and always shows up.

Who are They each to you?
How do you picture or see each of Them?
How do each of Them make you feel?

Next, a little 101 on how to take a deep breath.
Take deep breaths, preferably in and out through the nose (for sure on the in-breath), expanding that belly out on the in-breath and pulling it in on the out-breath. Focus your thoughts and center your heart with the help of these prompts.

So the first thing I do when it is time for my Jesus rests is I invite all Three into the time. On the in-breath, I think of and feel who each part of the Trinity is to me. And then on the out-breath, I say thank you to that part of the Trinity, and I ask Them to be here or lift the veil or show me what They need me to know or to speak and to help me understand.

Next, I take three more deep breaths, each one focused on part of the Trinity. On the in-breath, each part of Them tells me *I love you.* On the out-breath, I tell them I love you.
- In breath - Father says, I love you.
- Out breath - I tell Him, I love you.
- In breath - Jesus says, I love you.
- Out breath - I tell Him, I love you.
- In breath - Holy Spirit says, I love you.
- Out breath - I tell Her, I love you.

Finally, I practice gratitude breath prayers that are going to guide you through the sections of this book. My hope is that it is a daily reminder of the cover and comfort of our God who never leaves us.
- In breath - The Lord is my shepherd
- Out breath - I lack nothing.
- In breath - The Lord is my provider
- Out breath - thank you.
- In breath - The Lord is my protector
- Out breath - thank you.
- In breath - The Lord is my promise
- Out breath - thank you.
- In breath - The Lord is here, I am in Their presence
- Out breath - thank you.
- In breath - The Lord is my cover and comfort, I will praise
- Out breath - thank you.

Maybe this is where you stop most days because that is all your life allows right now. Perhaps you do just one of these breath prayers. No need to do them right, perfectly, in order, or anything close to what I have written above. These are to give you an idea of maybe where to begin and what I have found to be helpful.

Simply ask God, Jesus, and Holy Spirit to show up for you. Ask for Them to help you receive what you need that day.

And then rest and breathe.

May the vision devotions below help you to feel, see, and receive Them.

Just like breath prayers, there is no right or perfect way to read this devotional. Read it in one sitting like a story, relish in it over a few days, read one entry a day, read in order, pick a random page or anything in between.

My only ask is that you show up for yourself.
I promise, They will show up too.

Prologue

The threshing floor.

Surrounded by fields of wheat blowing in the pink and orange sunset winds, I walk onto the threshing floor where He waits for me with a look and deep sense of pride and love.
Daughter, you obeyed, look at what you did.

It is here I will repent for believing that control is my friend.

It is here I will praise all that He has done in, through, and for my life.

It is here I will work and worship in praise the opportunities He brings me because answering the call is how these fields were planted.

It is here I will rejoice in what will inevitably be the hard work, painful process, and the utterly, completely, and wholeheartedly worth it threshing and winnowing.

And then I will dance with my Jesus, feet on top of His, upon the threshing floor.

Provide

lies

My breath short.
The pain great.
The darkness begins to swallow me whole.

How is it possible to feel this alone?

I cry out for God to help me, quickly He says,
> *I am here, my child.*
> *Child, he is trying to get you to believe the old lies.*
> *Remember, I am here.*
> *Remember I will never leave you.*
> *Remember I know pain too.*
> *Remember I will use this.*
> *Remember.*

Scripture references:
Deuteronomy 7:9, Psalm 77:11, 2 Timothy 2:11-13

do it again

I scream at the enemy, you won't get me to believe the lies again!

My God is faithful. I am not being punished. And most of all He is with me.

I repeat it over and over as if to both sear it into my soul even more and to once and for all finally convince the darkness that this trick will no longer work on me.

I scream even louder. Keep trying you will not get me, and you will not win.

A full breath comes into me from nowhere, and I feel God there,
      Remember, child.

He loves me enough to be human like me.
He loves me enough to suffer and die for me.
He loves me enough to get me to Him.
He loves me enough to never leave me.

He is faithful. He is good. He never leaves me. He will win. He will do it again.

Scripture references:
Hebrews 10:23, Psalm 126:4, Philippians 2:6-8

up the hills

Jesus grabs my hand to lead me up the hill, with a twinkle in
His eye He says,
>   Come with me, I have something to show you, child.

The fields of wheat surround us, the harvest blowing in the
wind of Spirit.

Rolling hills warmed in the pinks, oranges, and purples of the
painted canvas of the sky.

We reach the hilltop and with a glance and a squeeze of my
hand I suddenly know this is what we've done, what we've
done together.

The harvest is here.

My promises are here, the promises of a God who always
provides.

They just aren't quite ready yet.
>   You, child, aren't quite ready yet.
>   That doesn't change my promises.
>   I promise.

Scripture references:
Isaiah 9:2-3, Psalm 126:5-6, James 3:18

the strength of roots

I'm playing with Jesus in the fields. Running back and forth, up and down, I point out the brightly colored butterflies with a squeal of childlike wonder. Bouncing back and forth with the dogs, a giggle escapes from somewhere in my soul I wasn't sure still existed.

I can't see my three, my babies who never breathed the earth's fresh air. Yet, I feel them somewhere amongst these hills of harvest.

Although I can feel the darkness easily overtake my joy as the storm has been tremendous and still feels ominous in the skies, the fields are ready to be claimed.

I also feel the power of God - here, present, covering, and providing.

Somewhere inside, somehow, I know He will use the storm. The clouds darken quickly again, the winds pick up, and the rains pound much of the fields down flat. Jesus keeps playing though, right alongside me. We are dry and encompassed in a bubble of light. It's then that I realize Spirit is there too, just there, like a light breeze around me.

They all notice my growing concern and trepidation, doubt settling in when suddenly the sky lights up with a rainbow.

They say,
> *We will use this, the harvest is there. Just a bit bent and weary. Do not question the strength in the roots and Our promise of the decree of Our time, the right time, and most of all Our care. The harvest is coming, child.*

Scripture references:
Jeremiah 17:7-8, Psalms 1:2-3, Colossians 2:7

you have the sword

Gertie, my cuddle bug dog, lays her head directly on top of the knot in my jaw and rubs along the tension for what feels like a few minutes. God, are we sure these dogs aren't your angels? I laugh as she makes eye contact with me as if winking and saying, of course we are, mom.

Suddenly, I am back shackled and silenced in pain, standing in front of Jesus, in our spot upon the threshing floor. Thick cuffs around both wrists with heavy chains up to another thick cuff around my throat. That isn't where it stops, though. From the cuff around my throat are more chains that lead to an impenetrable armor that goes around the back of my head, along my jaw and covers my mouth. There is a small suffocating grate for breath in front of my mouth. The armor is locked, tight, and painful - my eyes scared, breath short and shallow.

This is the floor I fought for my life months ago after a severe allergic reaction, the floor where I broke the contract of disappointment, the floor where Jesus has shown me the great harvest that is coming, and now the floor where I battle with the spirit of death, fear, hate and infirmity as it tries to stop me from speaking.

Jesus reminds me with a pull of His eyebrow and a quirky half-smile,
    "Remember, you have My sword."

I glance down and realize I am holding His sword of Spirit. My eyes are opened instantly to see the full armor upon me, *my* full armor of God, there this whole time.

I feel the heavy sword in my hand - looking down at it knowing I will never be able to lift it in my weary state. Jesus takes my armored jaw, chin in His hand, lifting my face to His just as the strength of Him courses through my body to lift the sword up to break off the opposite wrist chain. With a loud crash and a bright spark, together we lift it again breaking the other wrist free. And without a word from either of us, I take my hands up to my jaw - all the time looking at Jesus - ripping off the neck collar and jaw armor in one loud swoop. It crashes to the threshing floor with a loud clang.

"Am I possibly free? Without pain? Could it be?" I both ask and beg Him.

And with the same smirkish twinkle in His eyes, Jesus grins right as a mist rises from the threshing floor soaking me.
>   *Go.*
>   *Speak.*
>   *Go and water the earth.*

Scripture references:
Deuteronomy 8:3, Psalm 45:3, Ephesians 6:17

Protect

I will not be silenced

Listening to my friend Rebecca pray over me for the second time, I am overcome with breath-stealing sobs.

I see the shackles, chains, and armor again - none of it loosed. Not even a little. Tight and even more painful still, and I am getting scared.

I am scared.

I see and feel a mist come from the grate that is over my mouth in the armor around my jaw, as if no matter what the enemy tries, no matter how much pain, no matter how long this lasts, I will speak.

God will speak through me.

A mist of Spirit from me, the one who is shackled, in pain, and weary.

The pain is greater through the sobs, and fear settles into my soul as the pain only increases.
>*Remember, child, I will not be silenced.*

I can't do this like this, Father, I can't, I beg.
>*We will.*
>*Remember.*
>*From the beginning, a mist welled up from the earth and watered the whole face of the ground.*
>*Child, this is Me.*
>*This is Me in you.*
>*Drink up.*
>*Speak.*
>*Soak the earth.*
>*We will win.*

Scripture references:
Genesis 2:6, Isaiah 44:22

this is not of Me

The shackles are back.

Thick cuffs around both wrists, heavy chains up to another thick cuff around my throat.

Jesus stands before me, we're on the threshing floor again. We are surrounded by the fields of wheat He has shown me to be the promises of God's harvest for me.

It is dark and sunny at the same time, even though I don't understand how this is possible, and the air is thick.

I look at Jesus, unable to speak through the pain and fear, my eyes begging Him to help me. Jesus says,
> This is not of Me. This is not of you. Child, this is not a lie you are believing. Not an idol you've made. Not a punishment. And, not a fluke. This is not of this world. This is an attack to keep you quiet and in the darkness. This is not your truth. Your truth is of Me. Your truth is Me. This is not Me.

With a knowing of the dark spirit upon me, I try to breathe. I try to speak.

Only pain.

Suddenly I hear the gush of the summer sky open up with heavy rain even though now it seems to be sunny out. The concrete stones on the threshing floor steam, and that smirkish twinkle comes into Jesus' eyes again.

Jesus looks into me as I am soaked in the showers of his healing grace and love. The steel chains, bondages, and locks disintegrating with each raindrop. Nothing even left to be blown like chaff from the threshing floor. I am washed clean.

Only the steam rising up from the threshing floor.

A mist of Spirit.
Their mist.

Scripture references:
Isaiah 54:17, Psalm 91, Ephesians 6:12

chariots

"What about him?" I ask glancing first down at the now obliterated steel lock that was just on my jaw and is now in ash on the threshing floor and then looking beside me at the spirit of darkness.

> *"What about him? He doesn't stand a chance, my warrior child."*

Once again, They open my eyes. I see the chariots of fire, my armor, shield, and sword, my community of intercessors and healers, the fields full of harvest surrounding me, and His great angel armies.

Surrounded.
Surrounded in the fight.
Held in the pain.

The enemy can keep trying.

he has gotten me to believe his lies before, to contract with trauma, to believe I am invisible, to be too scared to speak, and to doubt the love and faithfulness of God.

he has nearly won, or so he has thought.

Not this time.
Not ever again.

the enemy's attempts to silence me, most of all to squelch the light of Jesus in me, are for naught because I am a stubborn ass, passionate, determined warrior child of the One True King. I have His healing power, love, and grace coursing through me under this armor, even if it includes painful chains on me right now.

His great Love, His great Grace, His great Light, and His great power in me will not be silenced.

> *Children, this is Me.*

This is Me in you.
Drink up.
Speak.
Soak the earth.

Scripture references:
2 Kings 6:17, Psalm 68:17, Matthew 24:30

He chuckles

The presence of God is overwhelming, it feels a little different than Jesus. Just as loving, just as present, the awe and power feels greater, though.

Reverberating around and through me.

Standing in front of God, I can feel His power.

I can also feel His delight and love in and for me.

Suddenly He takes and grabs the jaw and throat cuff that has been keeping me in pain and silent.

At first, I think and hope He will simply and easily crush it with His powerful love.

Instead, he takes it off me in one fell swoop and hits the spirit of darkness with it.

Then He chuckles, both at my surprise and at the darkness obliterated in His power.

Scripture references:
Exodus 14:14, Psalm 128:7, Romans 8:31

give them the sword

Tired.
Beat up.
Damn near done.
Weary.
So weary.
> Give your sword to them.
> Give yourself permission to ask your people to take the sword and slay the darkness for you for a bit.

Scripture references:
Ecclesiastes 4:9-10, Proverbs 17:17, Romans 12:10

we don't need a key

My friend Brooke prays and speaks and anoints my home and me. My body rushes with the warmth of Holy Spirit from head to toe as she lays hands on me praying in tongues.

The tension lifts.

Of course, it lifts a bit, satan is not welcome here, and he knows it.

I will speak. In pain still, with less fear and more knowing, I know I must keep going. As I begin working on this very book, the pain hits without warning. The jolt immediately sends pain into my skull, entire face, and down my neck. As if the enemy is saying, "don't even try," with each throb of pulsing pain.

Oh, how much he underestimates me and my Jesus.

I see the big steel lock on my jaw muscle, the knot that feels like it could literally take me deep down into the darkness and kill me.

The darkness tells me it is there forever, snarling at me, "See how much and how long you can really keep going. It is locked, and you don't have the key, and neither does your Savior".

"We don't need a fucking key!" I scream at the top of my lungs as I reach up with my left hand. My arm that is adorned with the birthstone butterflies of our would-be three babies. I grasp the cold lock tightly as it burns into the palm of my hand - darkness still fighting to win his battle. Looking back at Jesus, and with a smirk of knowing in both of us, I crush the lock off my jaw. The ash of the pulverized steel floats softly to the ground of the threshing floor through my tight fist.

Can it possibly be over? Please now, take this pain, God.

And Jesus says,

It was always over. It was over the day I loved you so much I died on the cross for you. Child, walk into this love, and receive your favor and anointed call.

Scripture reference:
Isaiah 53:5

take this cup

My cup of suffering.

Jesus takes the cup from my hands. At first, I think He'll drop it to the threshing floor into ash. Instead, He gives it to the darkness living on my left side.

He forces darkness to bow down to Him, the One True King, and drink from the very cup he has been using against me, thinking he could trample me to dust.

Except I am not dust.
I am light.

Scripture references:
Isaiah 51:22-23, Luke 22:42

strong enough

I am in God's armor.
It feels heavy today.
Almost too heavy to even carry.

How can that be?

Suddenly light drenches the threshing floor and me.
I feel all of Them - Father, Son, and Spirit.
Their presence and power.
Their love and light.
And mine too.
All coming from under the armor, the armor I thought I wasn't
strong enough to wear.

Scripture references:
Isaiah 59:17, Psalm 132:9, Romans 13:12

Promise

the cool breath

My head is searing in pain. Fire licks up the back of my head and along my lower jaw.

Jesus appears out of nowhere standing right in front of me. He reminds me He is always there, that He promises to never leave.

He glances up toward His right and with a mutual nod between Father and Son, as if the power is both shared between them and in them in their reckless love for me, I feel their breath.

With a simple and determined glance between Power and Love, I feel the cool breath of Them over me.

Fire cooled.
Pain calmed.
Peace received.

Scripture references:
Job 33:4, Psalm 104:29-30, 2 Timothy 3:16-17

let My light heal it

Praying for my healing and God interrupts,
>*No more rebuking, child.*
>*Bring My light in to heal.*
>*I will heal it.*
>*Ask Me to.*
>*See it.*
>*Feel Me.*
>*You aren't meant to walk this alone or battle yourself,*
>*and you don't have to.*
>*Give it to Me.*
>*Let Me bear it with you.*

>*Just like my Son and I said in the garden...*
>>*I don't want to, this is hard, I don't think I can do this, please take this cup.*

>***And**, I will. Not my will, Your will.*

>*We are together in this.*
>*We are with you.*

Scripture references:
Isaiah 58:8, Psalms 107:19-21, Matthew 5:34

can I have it?

He's always working on it, working on me, which really only means loving me.

He will wait. He will wait for me to turn to Him with it so He can sit beside me and say,
Me too child, Me too.

And then He'll ask,
Can I have it? Will you give Me this hurt?

And then, with a deep breath of equal parts faith and fear, I hand it over to Him. I hand it over to Him because of how I feel when He sees me. Because I can't possibly hold it myself any longer. Because I must.

Then He will wash it clean with His blood - gone with every last drop poured out for me (and for you).

He will then drop it to the threshing floor where it obliterates into ash like chaff that is both blown away with the mighty mother breath of Holy Spirit and washed away in God's crystal clear nourishing stream.

At first, I feel the breeze and watch the stream in disbelieving awe, and then I quickly remember that I am now bare - naked even. Looking down into my empty hands my brain tries to convince me of the lies of the world and shame.

Get it back. Now! You need it. You aren't enough just you. And you never will be. Take it back, you deserve that pain.

Then Her breeze brushes against my skin once more, and a random trickle from His cool stream somehow finds its way to my pinky toe, and I remember to look up.

I see Jesus, I *feel* Jesus. And He says,

Yes, you are, you are enough, especially with this, as he hands me a crown of purified gold and places it, not on my head, but around my heart.

I open my hands, open my heart, and receive His crown.

Scripture references:
Psalm 23:1, Proverbs 4:9, Luke 6:17, Philippian 4:19

scar healed by scar

My pain is less, it's different. I notice it through my smile just as Jesus takes His scarred hand and places it on top of my jaw picking up speed as He spins me around upon the threshing floor in a wild dance.

With a quiet crinkling sound the pain dissipates some. I look up at Him, smiling even bigger, feeling the warmth from His chest fill my whole body, just as He takes my left arm, the one adorned with the tattoo of my three, and places my hand over my own jaw.

His scarred hand on top of mine.
His pierced by darkness, mine by loss.
Scar upon scar.
Scar covered by scar.
Scar healed by scar.

Scripture references:
Job 5:18, 1 Peter 2:24, John 20:27

the place of your rise

He kisses me in a warm embrace where I feel it all - the glory and power of Father, the love and grace of Son, and the joy and breath of Spirit as if receiving the breath of life, new life, all over again.

Suddenly I realize, They've swept me up into another dance around the threshing floor, the threshing floor I once thought, for sure, would be the place of my demise.

And, with a soft touch of His hand to lift my face to His, Jesus reminds me,
> *Child, this is the place of your rise.*

Scripture references:
Isaiah 61:3, Psalm 87:7

the stronger armor

I feel heavy.
Weary.
How can I keep fighting?

And He says,
> *Don't forget your armor.*
> *Our armor is stronger than his shackles and chains.*
> *Allow the weight of that truth and courage to settle*
> *deeply into your very being and knowing, my child.*
> *You wear the armor always, you must remember it.*

Scripture references:
Psalm 18:17, 1 John 4:4

aroma of healing

Jesus is on my right, holding my hand. I notice He is holding a gold trumpet in His right hand as we stand on a hilltop of what I think and assume must be the fields of the coming harvest.

With a quick squeeze of my hand, He opens my eyes to see the fields begin to float up into the air as the wind picks up just a bit. I smell the sweet scent of milkweed flowers and see the seeds lift into the air with their white fluff floating everywhere.

Courage.
Grace.
Joy.
Forgiveness.
Empathy.
Connection.
Story.

I look to Jesus to see if He will help me understand.
> *Your story, which is our Truth, helps them to tell theirs. This is the aroma of healing for generations.*

And with that, the sun catches the gold trumpet in his hand and the land is washed bright with Love.

Scripture references:
2 Corinthians 2:15, 1 John 2:6, Galatians 2:20

Presence

inside out, outside in, always

Are you doing this? I ask Them.
> *Never child. I am allowing it.*

I glance at Jesus, who grabs my left hand.
> *We promise We will be here through all and always.*

I sense the dark infirmity lurking today in my neck.
God says,
> *It is him. And yes, I am letting it happen. Every time you suffer, We suffer. Every time you suffer, you grow more like Us because you turn more to Us and when you turn to Us more, someone sees Our light through you. Our love changes them - they fight for you in prayer. Your words of courage help them feel seen. Your tears help them feel strong enough to fight too. So yes, child, We will let this happen.*

No anger, no questioning, from me, not even the tiniest bit of it, only a little tug of desperation for more of Their presence.

I feel the panic strengthen as the enemy knows this is an easy way to get me to buy into his lies.

Instead, I turn more to Them begging Them never to leave me, to always open my eyes and show me, to cover me.

Jesus squeezes my hand even tighter as a warmth and calm fills me from the inside out and the outside in.
> *Always.*

Scripture references:
Hosea, 13:4, Joshua 1:9, Psalm 23:4, 1 Corinthians 3:16,

rest child

Jesus is sitting cross-legged on the threshing floor. He pats His lap. I curl up and lay my right side on His leg and He takes my left hand and places it on my jaw again. I can feel the cool air pass through His scarred hand while His hand heats up my whole face in a warmth that sends comfort throughout my whole body. He brushes my hair softly along my hairline with His right hand.

Rest, child, rest.

Scripture references:
Exodus 33:14, Psalm 4:8, Matthew 11:28

beat up wild

I feel God in the warm breeze following the storm.

My butterfly garden is full of yellows, pinks, purples, and every shade of green the eye can see, and God can create.

She is a bit wild.

And a little beat up following the torrential downpour and harsh winds.

And yet, with fresh drops of what she needs clinging to her leaves and petals.

Fighting to the light.
Daring to bloom.
She is resilient.
Always resilient.
She is the nourished peace after the storm.

Scripture references:
Isaiah 45:8, Job 37:6, Psalm 72:6, Matthew 6:28

carried

Jesus knows I am asking to crawl up in His lap again.
To be wrapped in His love.
Comforted.

Instead He takes me up.

My face on His chest, arms wrapped around one another.
Suddenly swept away, my feet on top of His.

Dancing.
Comforted.
Carried.
Loved.
In a dance.

Scripture references:
Isaiah 46:4, John 16:33, Romans 8:18

time to play

We're sitting like children cross-legged in a circle upon the threshing floor.

Jesus and God and me.
The sense of play in the air and between Them is palpable and yet too far away from me, especially in today's darkness.

Am I invited?

God takes my face in His hands and squeezing almost a bit too hard He says,
> *I am so proud. Keep fighting.*

Then Jesus places His scarred hand on my knee and leans forward,
> *I know it hurts.*

God leans in too,
> *We know, child.*

The complete sense of feeling understood, known, and loved envelopes everything of me.

There is room now.
They made room for the sparkle.
And I know it is now time to play.

Scripture references:
Psalm 126:2, Romans 12:15, Hebrews 4:15

especially in the dark

It's dark.
Around, and maybe even in.
> *I'm here. I am here even in and most especially when it is dark, child.*

Perhaps some of the darkness is cast by God's shadow covering us.

Scripture references:
Exodus 13:21-22, Psalm 36:7, James 1:17

blanket fort

Crawl on in.
Come play.
And rest.
The comfort and protection of God's shadow.
The truth and clarity of Jesus' flashlight.
The joyful play of Holy Spirit's storybooks and twinkle lights.
　　Cozy up here, child. It's a holy blanket fort.

Scripture references:
Isaiah 66:13, 2 Corinthians 1:3-4

throbbing

I remember in middle school, when a bully, or worse a friend, would take my forearm in both of their hands and twist their hands in opposite directions.

The pain of my skin being stretched in different directions and the hairs maybe even being pulled out.

I feel that now in my wrist as I type up this very book.

Maybe yours hurts too.
Or maybe it is your throat.
Or your back.
Or maybe even your heart.

This is darkness.
This is never of God.
He let me know this.

First, I had to feel the throbbing.
He then says,
> *Feel that throbbing, though? That is the heartbeat of Heaven coursing through and in you, child.*

Scripture references:
Isaiah 61:10, Psalm 51:12, John 15:1-8

fire

On earth as it is Heaven.
Heaven through me.

The light of heaven in and through me.

Even when it feels like fire, Lord?
> *Fire will come of this.*
> *The fire in your heart will ignite others.*
> *The chariots of fire and angel armies will protect it.*
> *And, I will breathe on it.*
> *Light up, child.*

Scripture references:
Exodus 24:17, Psalm 34:5, Matthew 5:16

Praise

live from that love

What if revival means the only thing we have in common is how loved we are by Him?
And how much we feel that love?
How much we live from that love?

To be brave enough to love as loved as we are.
To choose the courage to love all as He does.

What if this is revival?
The revival in the freedom to love all and sit beside like He did and does.
The revival grace of Jesus.

Scripture references:
Luke 6:35, John 13:34, John 15:13, 1 Peter 4:8, 1 John 4:7-8

you just have to ask

I want to see Heaven.
Lord, I need to see Heaven today.
　　You can see Heaven, child. You only have to ask.

Will you bring Heaven through me today Lord?
Will you bring Heaven to me here today?

Today I will choose to see God everywhere.
Living without the veil.
This is Heaven.

Scripture references:
Matthew 6:10, Revelation 21:1-5

pulled down into praise

The darkness keeps pulling.
Pulling down into what feels like the abyss of loss, fear, doubt,
of nothingness.

Am I here? Do I exist?

Does anyone hear me?
>   *I do, child.*

Keep pulling me down, I will not be swallowed by darkness.
Keep pulling me down, you will not win.
Keep pulling me down, the only place I will land is on my
knees praising my good Father and my Savior Jesus.

Scripture references:
Habakkuk 3:17-19, Psalm 34:1-4, Acts 16:25-26

playing with my three

With a quick glance from Him my eyes are suddenly opened to see them behind us playing amongst the fields of harvest on the hill. Their squeals of joy and laughter fill the air.

My three.
My three in *our* harvest.

Tears of great promise and forever wonder stream from my eyes.

No longer tears of fear and pain, the healing water flows through and from me into the waiting-for-harvest-fields.

The slight trickle soon gushes to a strong babble, which makes my three turn around looking back at our Jesus and me - their mama, upon the threshing floor.

With their smiles, the tear-filled streams rise up the hills towards them through the promised harvest Jesus and I have been planting for many years, the years since they were only born to Him.

We all stand in awe and wonder at the living water, the same awe and wonder I as their mama has for them every day, now an awe and wonder looking back at me.

With squeals and splashes, squished noses, and crinkled eyes my three look into me, as if saying, "We're okay, mama, we're better than okay, go and water the earth."

As quickly as we saw one another, they go back to playing, chasing, splashing, and laughing among the harvest and streams on the hillside.

Their happiness fills the air.
The babbling streams nourish the hills of harvest.
The rush of Spirit blowing through the fields heals.

And Love courses through it all.
Including me.

Scripture references:
Isaiah 44:3, Isaiah 54:1-6, Psalm 23:2, John 7:38-39

ABOUT THE AUTHOR

Justine is a Licensed Professional Counselor. For over seven years Justine has been certified in the work of Dr. Brené Brown. She has over 21 years of experience in traditional mental health and personal growth. Justine is the author of three best-selling books and was also honored to do TEDx Talks at TEDxUMDearborn and TEDxLaSierraUniversity. Currently, she travels nationally delivering keynotes, workshops, and trainings on topics such as leadership, courage, resilience, and much more. Justine lives in St. Louis with her husband Chad, their three dogs and for four months of the year hundreds of monarch butterflies.

Made in the USA
Monee, IL
02 September 2020